MAD LIBS®

YOU'VE GOT MAD LIBS

By Roger Price and Leonard Stern

Mad Libs
An Imprint of Penguin Random House

D1410903

MAD LIBS
Penguin Young Readers Group
An Imprint of Penguin Random House LLC

Mad Libs format and text copyright © 2004 by Penguin Random House LLC.
All rights reserved.

Concept created by Roger Price & Leonard Stern
Published by Mad Libs,
an imprint of Penguin Random House LLC,
345 Hudson Street, New York, New York 10014.
Printed in the USA.

ISBN 9780843108552
23 21 20 22 24

MAD LIBS is a registered trademark of Penguin Random House LLC.

MAD ☺ LIBS

INSTRUCTIONS

MAD LIBS® is a game for people who don't like games!
It can be played by one, two, three, four, or forty.

• RIDICULOUSLY SIMPLE DIRECTIONS

In this tablet you will find stories containing blank spaces where words are left out. One player, the READER, selects one of these stories. The READER does not tell anyone what the story is about. Instead, he/she asks the other players, the WRITERS, to give him/her words. These words are used to fill in the blank spaces in the story.

• TO PLAY

The READER asks each WRITER in turn to call out a word—an adjective or a noun or whatever the space calls for—and uses them to fill in the blank spaces in the story. The result is a MAD LIBS® game.

When the READER then reads the completed MAD LIBS® game to the other players, they will discover that they have written a story that is fantastic, screamingly funny, shocking, silly, crazy, or just plain dumb—depending upon which words each WRITER called out.

• EXAMPLE (*Before* and *After*)

" _____ !" he said _____
       EXCLAMATION   ADVERB

as he jumped into his convertible _____ and
                                      NOUN

drove off with his _____ wife.
                    ADJECTIVE

" *Ouch!* _____ !" he said *Stupidly* _____
       EXCLAMATION   ADVERB

as he jumped into his convertible *Cat* _____ and
                                        NOUN

drove off with his *brave* _____ wife.
                    ADJECTIVE

QUICK REVIEW

In case you have forgotten what adjectives, adverbs, nouns, and verbs are, here is a quick review:

An ADJECTIVE describes something or somebody. *Lumpy, soft, ugly, messy,* and *short* are adjectives.

An ADVERB tells how something is done. It modifies a verb and usually ends in "ly." *Modestly, stupidly, greedily,* and *carefully* are adverbs.

A NOUN is the name of a person, place, or thing. *Sidewalk, umbrella, bridle, bathtub,* and *nose* are nouns.

A VERB is an action word. *Run, pitch, jump,* and *swim* are verbs. Put the verbs in past tense if the directions say PAST TENSE. *Ran, pitched, jumped,* and *swam* are verbs in the past tense.

When we ask for A PLACE, we mean any sort of place: a country or city *(Spain, Cleveland)* or a room *(bathroom, kitchen).*

An EXCLAMATION or SILLY WORD is any sort of funny sound, gasp, grunt, or outcry, like *Wow!, Ouch!, Whomp!, Ick!,* and *Gadzooks!*

When we ask for specific words, like a NUMBER, a COLOR, an ANIMAL, or a PART OF THE BODY, we mean a word that is one of those things, like *seven, blue, horse,* or *head*.

When we ask for a PLURAL, it means more than one. For example, *cat* pluralized is *cats*.

MAD LIBS® is fun to play with friends, but you can also play it by yourself! To begin with, DO NOT look at the story on the page below. Fill in the blanks on this page with the words called for. Then, using the words you have selected, fill in the blank spaces in the story.

Now you've created your own hilarious MAD LIBS® game!

COMPUTER LAB

ADJECTIVE _____

NOUN _____

CELEBRITY (MALE) _____

NOUN _____

SOMETHING ALIVE _____

A PLACE _____

SAME CELEBRITY (MALE) _____

ADJECTIVE _____

PERSON IN ROOM (FEMALE) _____

ADJECTIVE _____

VERB ENDING IN "ING" _____

NOUN _____

VERB (PAST TENSE) _____

TOWN _____

PLURAL NOUN _____

NUMBER _____

SAME PLACE _____

TYPE OF FOOD (PLURAL) _____

NOUN _____

PLURAL NOUN _____

MAD LIBS
COMPUTER LAB

I love our computer lab at school. It's so _____!

ADJECTIVE

Every morning after _____ class, our teacher

NOUN

_____ takes us to the lab so we can work on cool

CELEBRITY (MALE)

class projects like finding out who is the oldest _____

NOUN

or what a/an _____ eats for breakfast. Last week, our

SOMETHING ALIVE

assignment was to research how many people live in the

_____. Since _____ always lets us pick our

A PLACE — SAME CELEBRITY (MALE)

_____ partners, I chose _____ because she's

ADJECTIVE — PERSON IN ROOM (FEMALE)

so _____. We had the best time _____ on the

ADJECTIVE — VERB ENDING IN "ING"

Internet. We found the coolest _____ that had all the

NOUN

information we needed. We _____ awesome facts about

VERB (PAST TENSE)

cities like _____ and all the _____ that live in

TOWN — PLURAL NOUN

them. Can you believe that _____ people live in

NUMBER

_____? And that they love to eat _____ for

SAME PLACE — TYPE OF FOOD (PLURAL)

breakfast, lunch, and _____? That's a lot of

NOUN

_____!

PLURAL NOUN

MAD LIBS® is fun to play with friends, but you can also play it by yourself! To begin with, DO NOT look at the story on the page below. Fill in the blanks on this page with the words called for. Then, using the words you have selected, fill in the blank spaces in the story.

Now you've created your own hilarious MAD LIBS® game!

HOW TO CLEAN YOUR COMPUTER

ADJECTIVE_____

ADVERB_____

VERB _____

NUMBER _____

ADJECTIVE_____

NOUN _____

ROOM _____

ADVERB_____

PLURAL NOUN _____

TYPE OF LIQUID _____

ADJECTIVE_____

PERSON IN ROOM (MALE)_____

ADJECTIVE_____

TYPE OF FOOD (PLURAL) _____

EXCLAMATION_____

PART OF THE BODY _____

VERB ENDING IN "ING" _____

VERB ENDING IN "ING" _____

SAME TYPE OF FOOD (PLURAL)_____

NOUN _____

ADJECTIVE_____

MAD LIBS®
HOW TO CLEAN YOUR COMPUTER

Since I use my computer every day, it can get _____

ADJECTIVE

really _____. I always make sure to _____ it

ADVERB   VERB

every _____ days in order to keep it shiny and _____. I'll

NUMBER   ADJECTIVE

grab a soft _____ from the _____ and

NOUN   ROOM

_____ wipe the keyboard down to get rid of all the

ADVERB

_____. Then I squirt some _____ on the screen to

PLURAL NOUN   TYPE OF LIQUID

get it nice and _____. This week, it was extra dirty because

ADJECTIVE

my little brother _____ decided to bring his

PERSON IN ROOM (MALE)

_____ plate of _____ into my room and eat it

ADJECTIVE   TYPE OF FOOD (PLURAL)

at my desk. When I yelled _____ and told him to stop, he

EXCLAMATION

stuck out his _____ at me and continued

PART OF THE BODY

_____. Then he started _____ so hard that

VERB ENDING IN "ING"   VERB ENDING IN "ING"

he spilled all of his _____ all over my

SAME TYPE OF FOOD (PLURAL)

_____. That is the last time I'll let my _____ little

NOUN   ADJECTIVE

brother in my room ever again!

MAD LIBS® is fun to play with friends, but you can also play it by yourself! To begin with, DO NOT look at the story on the page below. Fill in the blanks on this page with the words called for. Then, using the words you have selected, fill in the blank spaces in the story.

Now you've created your own hilarious MAD LIBS® game!

COMPUTERS ARE COOL

ADJECTIVE _____

PLURAL NOUN _____

NOUN _____

SOMETHING ALIVE (PLURAL) _____

VEHICLE _____

PLURAL NOUN _____

CELEBRITY (FEMALE) _____

CELEBRITY (MALE) _____

TYPE OF FOOD _____

SOMETHING ALIVE (PLURAL) _____

OCCUPATION _____

PLURAL NOUN _____

PLURAL NOUN _____

VERB ENDING IN "ING" _____

TYPE OF SPORT _____

PLURAL NOUN _____

MAD LIBS
COMPUTERS ARE COOL

Can you believe all of the _____ things you can do on a
ADJECTIVE

computer? You can find out anything—from where to buy the latest

_____ to how to make a delicious _____. I
PLURAL NOUN   NOUN

love to use my computer to find out cool facts like how many

_____ live in the ocean to tips on how to ride my
SOMETHING ALIVE (PLURAL)

cool _____. My older sister loves to surf the Web to find
VEHICLE

out how to paint her _____ and to learn the latest
PLURAL NOUN

gossip on _____ and _____. My mom
CELEBRITY (FEMALE)   CELEBRITY (MALE)

likes to use the computer too—she loves to find recipes for her

favorite _____ or how to grow beautiful
TYPE OF FOOD

_____ for our garden. But my dad uses the
SOMETHING ALIVE (PLURAL)

computer more than all of us put together! Since he's a/an

_____, he finds it useful to make _____ to
OCCUPATION   PLURAL NOUN

keep track of how many _____ his company is
PLURAL NOUN

_____. But sometimes I catch him looking up the
VERB ENDING IN "ING"

scores of his favorite _____ team, the _____.
TYPE OF SPORT   PLURAL NOUN

MAD LIBS® is fun to play with friends, but you can also play it by yourself! To begin with, DO NOT look at the story on the page below. Fill in the blanks on this page with the words called for. Then, using the words you have selected, fill in the blank spaces in the story.

Now you've created your own hilarious MAD LIBS® game!

INSTANT MESSAGING

YEAR _____

VERB _____

ADJECTIVE_____

CITY _____

FOREIGN COUNTRY _____

NOUN _____

ADJECTIVE_____

PERSON IN ROOM (FEMALE)_____

CELEBRITY (MALE) _____

TYPE OF SHOE (PLURAL) _____

ADJECTIVE_____

OCCUPATION _____

SAME PERSON IN ROOM (FEMALE) _____

NOUN _____

ADJECTIVE_____

SILLY NOISE _____

NOUN _____

VERB _____

MAD LIBS®
INSTANT MESSAGING

One of the coolest inventions of _____ is being able to

YEAR

_____ instant messages to your friends. It's _____!

VERB   ADJECTIVE

Since I have friends that live in _____ and _____,

CITY   FOREIGN COUNTRY

instant messaging is much cheaper than talking to them on the

_____. Usually, I only talk to each friend for a few minutes

NOUN

because I'm busy doing my_____ homework—unless

ADJECTIVE

_____ sends me a message. I can talk to her for

PERSON IN ROOM (FEMALE)

hours! We chat about everything from who is dating

_____ to what kind of _____ are the

CELEBRITY (MALE)   TYPE OF SHOE (PLURAL)

most _____. Since her mom works as a/an _____,

ADJECTIVE   OCCUPATION

_____ always has the latest gossip on the

SAME PERSON IN ROOM (FEMALE)

_____ industry. Isn't that _____? But my favorite

NOUN   ADJECTIVE

thing about instant messaging is the _____ my computer

SILLY NOISE

makes when my friend sends me a/an _____. It makes me

NOUN

_____ every time!

VERB

MAD LIBS® is fun to play with friends, but you can also play it by yourself! To begin with, DO NOT look at the story on the page below. Fill in the blanks on this page with the words called for. Then, using the words you have selected, fill in the blank spaces in the story.

Now you've created your own hilarious MAD LIBS® game!

MY COMPUTER

NOUN _____

YEAR _____

NOUN _____

A PLACE _____

COLOR_____

PLURAL NOUN _____

PLURAL NOUN _____

VERB _____

NOUN _____

PLURAL NOUN _____

A PLACE _____

PLURAL NOUN _____

ADJECTIVE_____

PERSON IN ROOM (FEMALE)_____

ADJECTIVE_____

VERB _____

MAD LIBS®
MY COMPUTER

I love my computer. It's my favorite _____ in the whole
                                        NOUN

world! I got it for my birthday in _____, and I've used it
                                    YEAR

every day since. It's in my bedroom on my _____, right
                                              NOUN

next to the window overlooking the _____. It's bright
                                       A PLACE

_____ with huge _____ hooked up to it
      COLOR   PLURAL NOUN

so I can listen to the latest CD from my favorite band, the

_____. The first thing I do when I _____ down
   PLURAL NOUN   VERB

at my computer is check the day's weather _____.
                                              NOUN

Then I'll go see what's happening in the day's local

_____. And since our family is taking a vacation to
   PLURAL NOUN

_____, I usually go on their website to see what kind of
     A PLACE

fun _____ are happening there. Sometimes my
        PLURAL NOUN

_____ little sister _____ tries to come
      ADJECTIVE   PERSON IN ROOM (FEMALE)

in and use my computer, but I never let her! She's so

_____ that I'm afraid she'll _____ it.
      ADJECTIVE   VERB

MAD LIBS® is fun to play with friends, but you can also play it by yourself! To begin with, DO NOT look at the story on the page below. Fill in the blanks on this page with the words called for. Then, using the words you have selected, fill in the blank spaces in the story.

Now you've created your own hilarious MAD LIBS® game!

SURF'S UP!

VERB (PAST TENSE)_____

ADJECTIVE_____

NUMBER _____

VERB _____

ADJECTIVE_____

VERB _____

NOUN _____

NOUN _____

ADJECTIVE_____

SILLY WORD_____

NOUN _____

PART OF THE BODY _____

PLURAL NOUN _____

FOREIGN COUNTRY _____

ARTICLE OF CLOTHING (PLURAL)_____

VERB ENDING IN "ING" _____

VERB ENDING IN "ING" _____

MAD LIBS

SURF'S UP!

If you've never _____ the Web before, it can be quite
         VERB (PAST TENSE)

_____. My mom found it so hard that it took me
  ADJECTIVE

_____ hours to _____ her! Here are some
  NUMBER   VERB

_____ tips on how to correctly _____ your
  ADJECTIVE   VERB

way through!

- You'll first need to make sure you have _____ access.
              NOUN

  This will enable you to connect to your favorite _____.
              NOUN

- You'll need to pick a/an _____ engine to find the
         ADJECTIVE

  information you're looking for. My favorite is _____.
              SILLY WORD

- Now the _____ begins! You'll be able to look up any
      NOUN

  information your _____ desires! From learning about
        PART OF THE BODY

  popular _____ in _____ to shopping for
       PLURAL NOUN   FOREIGN COUNTRY

  _____, the Web is yours!
  ARTICLE OF CLOTHING (PLURAL)

- After you've finished _____, make sure to log off
       VERB ENDING IN "ING"

  correctly. Your computer needs a break after all that

  _____!
  VERB ENDING IN "ING"

MAD LIBS® is fun to play with friends, but you can also play it by yourself! To begin with, DO NOT look at the story on the page below. Fill in the blanks on this page with the words called for. Then, using the words you have selected, fill in the blank spaces in the story.

Now you've created your own hilarious MAD LIBS® game!

KEYBOARDING TIPS

NUMBER _____

FOREIGN COUNTRY _____

ADVERB_____

VERB ENDING IN "ING" _____

PART OF THE BODY (PLURAL) _____

PLURAL NOUN _____

TYPE OF BUILDING _____

ADJECTIVE_____

PART OF THE BODY (PLURAL) _____

SAME PART OF THE BODY (PLURAL)_____

PLURAL NOUN _____

VERB ENDING IN "ING" _____

NUMBER _____

PLURAL NOUN _____

VERB _____

PLURAL NOUN _____

LANGUAGE _____

NOUN _____

MAD LIBS®
KEYBOARDING TIPS

Since you'll most likely be on your computer for _____ hours
                                                    NUMBER

a day, it's very important that you learn how to type quickly. That

way, you'll be able to finish your research project on _____
                                                       FOREIGN COUNTRY

_____ and amaze your friends with your _____
   ADVERB   VERB ENDING IN "ING"

skills! Since my _____ would never land on the
                  PART OF THE BODY (PLURAL)

_____ correctly, I decided to take a keyboarding class
   PLURAL NOUN

at my local _____. My teacher was _____!
            TYPE OF BUILDING   ADJECTIVE

The first thing he told me to do was to properly position my

_____ on the keyboard. Then he showed me how
PART OF THE BODY (PLURAL)

to move my _____ to be able to type actual
           SAME PART OF THE BODY (PLURAL)

_____! I practiced my _____ skills every
   PLURAL NOUN   VERB ENDING IN "ING"

night until I could type _____ words a minute! All of my
                          NUMBER

_____ are so jealous—I _____ so fast that I am
   PLURAL NOUN   VERB

always the first one to finish typing my _____ for
                                          PLURAL NOUN

_____ class. All those hours of hard _____
   LANGUAGE   NOUN

were worth it!

MAD LIBS® is fun to play with friends, but you can also play it by yourself! To begin with, DO NOT look at the story on the page below. Fill in the blanks on this page with the words called for. Then, using the words you have selected, fill in the blank spaces in the story.

Now you've created your own hilarious MAD LIBS® game!

COMPUTER DECORATING

ADJECTIVE_____

PLURAL NOUN _____

VERB _____

ADJECTIVE_____

ADJECTIVE_____

CELEBRITY (MALE) _____

ADJECTIVE_____

NOUN _____

ADJECTIVE_____

TYPE OF SPORT _____

NOUN _____

VERB _____

ADVERB_____

NAME OF PERSON (FEMALE)_____

NOUN _____

A PLACE _____

ADJECTIVE_____

PERSON IN ROOM (FEMALE)_____

COLOR_____

PLURAL NOUN _____

ADJECTIVE_____

MAD LIBS

COMPUTER DECORATING

One of the most _____ things about having your own
ADJECTIVE

computer is that you get to decorate it any way you want. I bought

the coolest _____ to _____ all over the
PLURAL NOUN   VERB

monitor—it looks so _____! Then I have a selection of
ADJECTIVE

my most _____ screen savers. My favorite one is a
ADJECTIVE

picture of _____, the most _____ actor of
CELEBRITY (MALE)   ADJECTIVE

all time. I can look at his _____ for hours! Sometimes
NOUN

when I'm working on a/an _____ project, like doing a
ADJECTIVE

report on _____, I minimize my _____ so I can
TYPE OF SPORT   NOUN

_____ _____ at him. My friend _____
VERB   ADVERB   NAME OF PERSON (FEMALE)

has a screen saver of a beautiful _____ in
NOUN

_____. She said that when she looks at it, it makes her
A PLACE

feel so _____. But do you know what my friend
ADJECTIVE

_____ put on her computer? She bought the cutest
PERSON IN ROOM (FEMALE)

_____ _____ and lined them up all over the top of the
COLOR   PLURAL NOUN

monitor. Isn't that so _____?
ADJECTIVE

From YOU'VE GOT MAD LIBS® • Copyright © 2004 by Penguin Random House LLC.

MAD LIBS® is fun to play with friends, but you can also play it by yourself! To begin with, DO NOT look at the story on the page below. Fill in the blanks on this page with the words called for. Then, using the words you have selected, fill in the blank spaces in the story.

Now you've created your own hilarious MAD LIBS® game!

MY LAPTOP

PERSON IN ROOM (MALE)_____

ADJECTIVE_____

EXCLAMATION_____

NOUN _____

NUMBER _____

A PLACE _____

ADJECTIVE_____

VERB _____

COLOR_____

NUMBER _____

VERB ENDING IN "ING" _____

A PLACE _____

ADJECTIVE_____

NOUN _____

A PLACE _____

PART OF THE BODY_____

LANGUAGE _____

PLURAL NOUN _____

SAME PERSON IN ROOM (MALE) _____

VERB _____

MAD LIBS
MY LAPTOP

Guess what Uncle _____ got me for my birthday? A/An
<u>PERSON IN ROOM (MALE)</u>

_____ new laptop! When I opened it, I yelled
<u>ADJECTIVE</u>

_____ and gave him a great, big _____. He
<u>EXCLAMATION</u> <u>NOUN</u>

said since I just turned _____ years old, it was important that I
<u>NUMBER</u>

have my own laptop in order to do better in my classes at

_____. My laptop is so _____ that I can
<u>A PLACE</u> <u>ADJECTIVE</u>

_____ it anywhere. It's bright _____ and weighs
<u>VERB</u> <u>COLOR</u>

_____ pounds. It even has a sleek _____
<u>NUMBER</u> <u>VERB ENDING IN "ING"</u>

case, so I can take it to the _____ with me. Isn't that
<u>A PLACE</u>

_____? Now I can lie down on the _____,
<u>ADJECTIVE</u> <u>NOUN</u>

look at the beautiful sparkling _____, and get a tan on
<u>A PLACE</u>

my _____ while I type up my project for
<u>PART OF THE BODY</u>

_____ class. But I have to be careful not to get
<u>LANGUAGE</u>

_____ in my laptop—Uncle _____ would
<u>PLURAL NOUN</u> <u>SAME PERSON IN ROOM (MALE)</u>

_____ me!
<u>VERB</u>

MAD LIBS® is fun to play with friends, but you can also play it by yourself! To begin with, DO NOT look at the story on the page below. Fill in the blanks on this page with the words called for. Then, using the words you have selected, fill in the blank spaces in the story.

Now you've created your own hilarious MAD LIBS® game!

E-MAIL ETIQUETTE

VERB ENDING IN "ING" _____

CITY _____

LANGUAGE _____

ADJECTIVE _____

ADJECTIVE _____

VERB ENDING IN "ING" _____

PLURAL NOUN _____

VERB ENDING IN "ING" _____

VERB _____

ADJECTIVE _____

VERB _____

VERB ENDING IN "ING" _____

ADJECTIVE _____

PLURAL NOUN _____

PLURAL NOUN _____

ADVERB _____

TYPE OF FOOD (PLURAL) _____

ADJECTIVE _____

MAD LIBS®
E-MAIL ETIQUETTE

When _____ to your relatives in _____ or to
    VERB ENDING IN "ING"   CITY

your _____ teacher, it's _____ to make your
      LANGUAGE   ADJECTIVE

e-mails as simple and _____ as possible. Here are the
                    ADJECTIVE

following tips for _____ the perfect e-mail:
          VERB ENDING IN "ING"

• Make sure that you don't write in all capital _____—it
                            PLURAL NOUN

  will sound like you're _____.
              VERB ENDING IN "ING"

• It's important to _____ your words correctly. Otherwise,
             VERB

  people will think you are _____ and that you don't
                 ADJECTIVE

  take enough time to _____ your e-mails before you send them.
             VERB

• Write to someone as if you're actually _____ to them. It's
                  VERB ENDING IN "ING"

  very _____ to write in incomplete _____ and
      ADJECTIVE   PLURAL NOUN

  use the wrong _____.
         PLURAL NOUN

• Try to get to the point of your e-mail as _____ as
                    ADVERB

  possible. Since many people don't even have the time anymore to sit

  down and eat _____ with their families, be as
         TYPE OF FOOD (PLURAL)

  _____ with your e-mails as possible.
  ADJECTIVE

MAD LIBS® is fun to play with friends, but you can also play it by yourself! To begin with, DO NOT look at the story on the page below. Fill in the blanks on this page with the words called for. Then, using the words you have selected, fill in the blank spaces in the story.

Now you've created your own hilarious MAD LIBS® game!

COMPUTER VIRUS

NOUN _____

VERB _____

ADJECTIVE _____

NOUN _____

NOUN _____

ADVERB _____

EXCLAMATION _____

VERB _____

OCCUPATION _____

NOUN _____

VERB ENDING IN "ING" _____

SILLY WORD _____

ADJECTIVE _____

TOWN _____

NOUN _____

PLURAL NOUN _____

ADJECTIVE _____

MAD LIBS
COMPUTER VIRUS

I hate it when I'm working on an important _____ and
                                                    NOUN

suddenly my computer decides to _____. It's so
                                         VERB

_____! Last time, I was putting the finishing touches
      ADJECTIVE

on my final _____ for my _____ class when
                   NOUN   NOUN

_____ my computer screen went blank. I yelled
      ADVERB

_____ and almost started to _____. Luckily,
   EXCLAMATION   VERB

my dad works as a/an _____, so he rushed right in and
                          OCCUPATION

helped me retrieve my lost _____. He said it happened
                                  NOUN

because of a computer virus that was _____ around
                                          VERB ENDING IN "ING"

cyberspace. It was named _____ and was rumored to be
                              SILLY WORD

started by some _____ kids in _____. Luckily,
                    ADJECTIVE   TOWN

he had a software _____ that will help protect my
                        NOUN

computer against any nasty _____ in the future. Isn't my
                                PLURAL NOUN

dad the most _____ dad ever?
                  ADJECTIVE

MAD LIBS® is fun to play with friends, but you can also play it by yourself! To begin with, DO NOT look at the story on the page below. Fill in the blanks on this page with the words called for. Then, using the words you have selected, fill in the blank spaces in the story.

Now you've created your own hilarious MAD LIBS® game!

COMPUTER PARTS

NOUN _____

ADJECTIVE _____

NUMBER _____

ADJECTIVE _____

NOUN _____

PART OF THE BODY _____

VERB ENDING IN "ING" _____

ADJECTIVE _____

PLURAL NOUN _____

NOUN _____

ADJECTIVE _____

PLURAL NOUN _____

CELEBRITY (FEMALE) _____

ADJECTIVE _____

PERSON IN ROOM (FEMALE) _____

ANIMAL _____

A PLACE _____

ADVERB _____

MAD LIBS
COMPUTER PARTS

Even though a computer looks like a simple piece of

_____, it's actually very _____.
NOUN ADJECTIVE

There are over _____ parts to it! One of the most
NUMBER

_____ parts to a computer is the CPU, which stands
ADJECTIVE

for Central Processing _____. It's actually considered the
NOUN

_____ of the computer, where all the computer's
PART OF THE BODY

_____ is done. The computer's hard drive is also very
VERB ENDING IN "ING"

_____—it's where all of the computer's
ADJECTIVE

_____ are contained. Then there is the computer's
PLURAL NOUN

monitor, which looks like a television _____ but is a lot
NOUN

more _____. The computer's keyboard contains all of
ADJECTIVE

the _____ that enable you to write a letter to
PLURAL NOUN

_____ or to your _____ aunt _____.
CELEBRITY (FEMALE)   ADJECTIVE   PERSON IN ROOM (FEMALE)

But my favorite part of the computer is the _____. It allows
ANIMAL

you to navigate your way through _____ and find the
A PLACE

information you need quickly and _____.
ADVERB

MAD LIBS® is fun to play with friends, but you can also play it by yourself! To begin with, DO NOT look at the story on the page below. Fill in the blanks on this page with the words called for. Then, using the words you have selected, fill in the blank spaces in the story.

Now you've created your own hilarious MAD LIBS® game!

START YOUR ENGINES!

NUMBER _____

NOUN _____

PLURAL NOUN _____

ADJECTIVE _____

VERB _____

SILLY WORD _____

FIRST NAME (MALE) _____

SILLY WORD _____

ADJECTIVE _____

VERB _____

ADVERB _____

CELEBRITY (FEMALE) _____

OCCUPATION _____

VERB _____

PLURAL NOUN _____

OCCUPATION _____

MAD LIBS
START YOUR ENGINES!

There are over _____ ways to look up information on
NUMBER

the Internet. But before you can get to your favorite website on how

to play the _____ or where to buy _____,
NOUN   PLURAL NOUN

you need to have a/an _____ search engine that will
ADJECTIVE

help you _____ for the information. My favorite search
VERB

engine is _____, but my friend _____ likes to
SILLY WORD   FIRST NAME (MALE)

use _____ instead. He says it's faster and more
SILLY WORD

_____. A search engine will _____ you to
ADJECTIVE   VERB

find what you are looking for _____ and efficiently. My
ADVERB

computer teacher _____ says a search engine is almost
CELEBRITY (FEMALE)

like a/an _____ in the sense that it helps you
OCCUPATION

_____ through a lot of information and helps you find
VERB

the most important _____. I knew she was my favorite
PLURAL NOUN

_____ for a reason!
OCCUPATION

MAD LIBS® is fun to play with friends, but you can also play it by yourself! To begin with, DO NOT look at the story on the page below. Fill in the blanks on this page with the words called for. Then, using the words you have selected, fill in the blank spaces in the story.

Now you've created your own hilarious MAD LIBS® game!

CHAT ROOMS

ADJECTIVE _____

YEAR _____

FOREIGN COUNTRY _____

PERSON IN ROOM (MALE) _____

NOUN _____

VERB _____

SILLY WORD _____

NUMBER _____

PLURAL NOUN _____

CELEBRITY (MALE) _____

NOUN _____

ADJECTIVE _____

VERB _____

EXCLAMATION _____

ADJECTIVE _____

VERB ENDING IN "ING" _____

CELEBRITY (FEMALE) _____

ADVERB _____

VERB ENDING IN "ING" _____

NOUN _____

ADVERB _____

MAD LIBS®
CHAT ROOMS

One of the most _____ inventions of _____ is the
                    ADJECTIVE   YEAR

creation of chat rooms. You can talk to people as far away as

_____ or to your friend _____ from
FOREIGN COUNTRY   PERSON IN ROOM (MALE)

_____ class. My favorite room to _____ in
NOUN   VERB

is called _____, where my friends and I log on every night
          SILLY WORD

at _____ o'clock and discuss what happened on our
   NUMBER

favorite TV show, _The_ _____. _____ is
                       PLURAL NOUN   CELEBRITY (MALE)

our favorite character on the _____. He is so
                              NOUN

_____ that he makes us want to _____
ADJECTIVE   VERB

_____! We're so _____ while we're chatting
EXCLAMATION   ADJECTIVE

that sometimes we end up _____ all at once! Since my
                         VERB ENDING IN "ING"

friend _____ types _____, she always
       CELEBRITY (FEMALE)   ADVERB

ends up _____ the most. But ever since I took
        VERB ENDING IN "ING"

a keyboarding _____, I can type almost as
              NOUN

_____ as she can!
ADVERB

MAD LIBS® is fun to play with friends, but you can also play it by yourself! To begin with, DO NOT look at the story on the page below. Fill in the blanks on this page with the words called for. Then, using the words you have selected, fill in the blank spaces in the story.

Now you've created your own hilarious MAD LIBS® game!

SHOP TILL YOU DROP!

VERB _____

ADJECTIVE _____

FOREIGN COUNTRY _____

A PLACE _____

VERB _____

PLURAL NOUN _____

VERB _____

FIRST NAME (FEMALE) _____

CELEBRITY (MALE) _____

ANIMAL _____

SILLY WORD _____

SOMETHING ALIVE (PLURAL) _____

TYPE OF FOOD (PLURAL) _____

VERB _____

VERB _____

SILLY WORD _____

NOUN _____

VERB _____

TYPE OF FOOD (PLURAL) _____

VERB (PAST TENSE) _____

VERB ENDING IN "ING" _____

MAD LIBS

SHOP TILL YOU DROP!

One of the coolest things about the Internet is that you can

_____ from home! It's so _____! Since
      VERB   ADJECTIVE

most of my family lives in _____ or _____,
          FOREIGN COUNTRY   A PLACE

it's a great way to _____ them their favorite
           VERB

_____. My mom will _____ at the
  PLURAL NOUN   VERB

computer for hours, ordering gifts for my aunt _____,
                FIRST NAME (FEMALE)

_____, and even my uncle's _____,
  CELEBRITY (MALE)   ANIMAL

_____! She will usually pick an assortment of fresh
  SILLY WORD

_____ or yummy _____, because
 SOMETHING ALIVE (PLURAL)   TYPE OF FOOD (PLURAL)

they tend to _____ well. My dad, however, loves to
         VERB

_____ on the Internet only for himself. Last week he
  VERB

went on his favorite website, _____.com, and bought a
            SILLY WORD

giant _____ so he can _____ his favorite
    NOUN   VERB

barbecued _____. Even though my mom
    TYPE OF FOOD (PLURAL)

_____ at him, there's no _____ when he's
 VERB (PAST TENSE)   VERB ENDING IN "ING"

shopping online!

MAD LIBS® is fun to play with friends, but you can also play it by yourself! To begin with, DO NOT look at the story on the page below. Fill in the blanks on this page with the words called for. Then, using the words you have selected, fill in the blank spaces in the story.

Now you've created your own hilarious MAD LIBS® game!

HOMEWORK HELP

NOUN _____

VERB ENDING IN "ING" _____

PLURAL NOUN _____

PART OF THE BODY (PLURAL) _____

FOREIGN COUNTRY _____

PLURAL NOUN _____

VERB _____

ADJECTIVE_____

NUMBER _____

NUMBER _____

SILLY WORD_____

VERB ENDING IN "ING" _____

A PLACE _____

PLURAL NOUN _____

VERB ENDING IN "ING" _____

ADJECTIVE_____

VERB ENDING IN "ING" _____

VERB ENDING IN "ING" _____

MAD LIBS

HOMEWORK HELP

One of the best things about having your own _____ is
                                                   NOUN

that _____ your homework is so much easier! All the
        VERB ENDING IN "ING"

_____ you need are right at your _____!
PLURAL NOUN   PART OF THE BODY (PLURAL)

Last week, I had to research the country of _____ and
                                               FOREIGN COUNTRY

all the _____ that _____ there. With my
         PLURAL NOUN   VERB

_____ computer, it was no problem at all! I was able to
ADJECTIVE

access _____ different websites at once! And it only
        NUMBER

took _____ minutes! My teacher Mr. _____,
      NUMBER   SILLY WORD

however, warns our class that the Internet should not be used for

_____, and that we should also go to the
VERB ENDING IN "ING"

_____ and read actual _____ instead of
A PLACE   PLURAL NOUN

spending all of our time _____ the Web. So along with
                          VERB ENDING IN "ING"

my _____ share of _____ on my
     ADJECTIVE   VERB ENDING IN "ING"

computer, I also spend a lot of time _____ in the
                                      VERB ENDING IN "ING"

library, the old-fashioned way!

MAD LIBS® is fun to play with friends, but you can also play it by yourself! To begin with, DO NOT look at the story on the page below. Fill in the blanks on this page with the words called for. Then, using the words you have selected, fill in the blank spaces in the story.

Now you've created your own hilarious MAD LIBS® game!

COMPUTER CLASS

ADJECTIVE_____

NUMBER _____

ADJECTIVE_____

CELEBRITY (FEMALE)_____

FOREIGN COUNTRY _____

SILLY WORD_____

ADJECTIVE_____

SOMETHING ALIVE (PLURAL) _____

VERB _____

VERB _____

PLURAL NOUN _____

NOUN _____

VERB _____

PLURAL NOUN _____

VERB (PAST TENSE)_____

LAST NAME OF PERSON _____

SILLY WORD_____

MAD LIBS
COMPUTER CLASS

Every _____ morning at _____ o'clock, I
       ADJECTIVE   NUMBER

have a computer class. At first I thought it would be totally

_____, but, boy, was I wrong! I get to sit next to
ADJECTIVE

_____, my best friend in all of _____. My
CELEBRITY (FEMALE)   FOREIGN COUNTRY

favorite teacher, Ms. _____, teaches the class, which
                  SILLY WORD

makes it so _____. She brings in delicious
          ADJECTIVE

_____ to _____ while she teaches us
SOMETHING ALIVE (PLURAL)   VERB

how computers _____ and how they can teach us so
          VERB

many different _____. Sometimes she gives us a typing
        PLURAL NOUN

_____ to see how fast we can _____ an e-mail,
NOUN   VERB

and other times she lets us speak about our very favorite

_____. Just when I thought our class couldn't get any
PLURAL NOUN

better, she _____ Bill _____ to speak to
      VERB (PAST TENSE)   LAST NAME OF PERSON

us about his computer company, _____. I wish I could
                        SILLY WORD

go to computer class every day!

MAD LIBS® is fun to play with friends, but you can also play it by yourself! To begin with, DO NOT look at the story on the page below. Fill in the blanks on this page with the words called for. Then, using the words you have selected, fill in the blank spaces in the story.

Now you've created your own hilarious MAD LIBS® game!

INTERNET FACTS

VERB (PAST TENSE)_____

YEAR _____

ADJECTIVE_____

CELEBRITY (MALE)_____

CELEBRITY (FEMALE) _____

VERB _____

NOUN _____

VERB _____

NOUN _____

NUMBER _____

VERB ENDING IN "ING" _____

VERB ENDING IN "ING" _____

NUMBER _____

NUMBER _____

PERSON IN ROOM (FEMALE)_____

TYPE OF FOOD (PLURAL) _____

NUMBER _____

PLURAL NOUN _____

ADJECTIVE_____

MAD LIBS
INTERNET FACTS

- The Internet was _____ in _____. Isn't that

  _____?
  ADJECTIVE
  VERB (PAST TENSE)   YEAR

- The Internet was originally called the ARPAnet, and was developed

  by _____ and _____ in order
  CELEBRITY (MALE)   CELEBRITY (FEMALE)

  to _____ the possibility of a computer _____
  VERB   NOUN

  that would be able to _____ a/an _____.
  VERB   NOUN

- On average, people spend up to _____ hours a year
  NUMBER

  _____ the Web. That's a lot of _____!
  VERB ENDING IN "ING"   VERB ENDING IN "ING"

- The fastest growing group of Internet users are aged _____ to
  NUMBER

  _____. No wonder Grandma _____ doesn't
  NUMBER   PERSON IN ROOM (FEMALE)

  have time to make _____ anymore!
  TYPE OF FOOD (PLURAL)

- There are over _____ million Web _____
  NUMBER   PLURAL NOUN

  available. That's so _____!
  ADJECTIVE

MAD LIBS® is fun to play with friends, but you can also play it by yourself! To begin with, DO NOT look at the story on the page below. Fill in the blanks on this page with the words called for. Then, using the words you have selected, fill in the blank spaces in the story.

Now you've created your own hilarious MAD LIBS® game!

HOW TO MAKE YOUR OWN WEBSITE

ADJECTIVE _____

VERB _____

PERSON IN ROOM (MALE) _____

ADJECTIVE _____

VERB (PAST TENSE) _____

VERB ENDING IN "ING" _____

PLURAL NOUN _____

VERB _____

ADJECTIVE _____

PLURAL NOUN _____

VERB _____

ADJECTIVE _____

SILLY WORD _____

CELEBRITY (MALE) _____

SOMETHING ALIVE (PLURAL) _____

ANIMAL _____

SILLY WORD _____

NUMBER _____

MAD LIBS
HOW TO MAKE YOUR OWN WEBSITE

It might sound very _____ to _____ your
                          ADJECTIVE   VERB

own website, but it's actually pretty simple. My friend

_____ knows everything about computers, so he
PERSON IN ROOM (MALE)

taught me all the _____ rules. It's important to have a
                        ADJECTIVE

basic understanding of HTML—which is the language that web

pages are _____ into. Otherwise, your computer will
           VERB (PAST TENSE)

have trouble _____ you. HTML consists of a series of
             VERB ENDING IN "ING"

_____ that are abbreviations for what they
PLURAL NOUN

_____ for. They're really _____ to learn.
VERB   ADJECTIVE

Once you have the _____ down, you'll be ready
                      PLURAL NOUN

to _____! You can fill your own website with
       VERB

so many _____ things! On my website
            ADJECTIVE

_____.com, I have pictures of _____, a list
SILLY WORD   CELEBRITY (MALE)

of my favorite _____, and a picture of my pet
               SOMETHING ALIVE (PLURAL)

_____, _____. And it only took me
ANIMAL   SILLY WORD

_____ minutes to do!
NUMBER

MAD LIBS® is fun to play with friends, but you can also play it by yourself! To begin with, DO NOT look at the story on the page below. Fill in the blanks on this page with the words called for. Then, using the words you have selected, fill in the blank spaces in the story.

Now you've created your own hilarious MAD LIBS® game!

CHAT EMOTICONS

PERSON IN ROOM (FEMALE)_____

FIRST NAME (FEMALE) _____

FOREIGN COUNTRY _____

ADJECTIVE_____

TYPE OF SPORT _____

LANGUAGE _____

ANIMAL _____

ADJECTIVE_____

PART OF THE BODY _____

PERSON IN ROOM (MALE)_____

ADJECTIVE_____

NOUN _____

PART OF THE BODY _____

SILLY NOISE _____

VERB _____

PLURAL NOUN _____

LANGUAGE _____

MAD LIBS
CHAT EMOTICONS

When writing an e-mail to your best friend _____

                                                      PERSON IN ROOM (FEMALE)

or your favorite aunt _____ in _____, you

                         FIRST NAME (FEMALE)   FOREIGN COUNTRY

can use the most _____ symbols instead of words! This

                          ADJECTIVE

way, you won't have to type so many words and instead can play

_____ or study for your _____ exam. And

TYPE OF SPORT   LANGUAGE

it's fun too! For example, instead of using the word

"_____" you can use (:V instead. Isn't that

            ANIMAL

_____? If you want to tell someone that they have a big

ADJECTIVE

_____, you can write :(). My best friend,

PART OF THE BODY

_____, is always _____, so he's always

PERSON IN ROOM (MALE)   ADJECTIVE

using the :) symbol. My favorite _____ to use is :P,

                                    NOUN

which means sticking out your _____. Every time I

                                PART OF THE BODY

type it, I always make a/an _____ and _____

                         SILLY NOISE   VERB

out loud! Sometimes I use so many _____ that I forget

                              PLURAL NOUN

they're not really _____!

            LANGUAGE

MAD LIBS® is fun to play with friends, but you can also play it by yourself! To begin with, DO NOT look at the story on the page below. Fill in the blanks on this page with the words called for. Then, using the words you have selected, fill in the blank spaces in the story.

Now you've created your own hilarious MAD LIBS® game!

AWESOME ABBREVIATIONS

PLURAL NOUN _____

VERB _____

NUMBER _____

VERB (PAST TENSE) _____

ADJECTIVE _____

VERB _____

ADJECTIVE _____

NUMBER _____

CELEBRITY (FEMALE) _____

VERB ENDING IN "ING" _____

VERB _____

EXCLAMATION _____

ADJECTIVE _____

SOMETHING ALIVE _____

ADJECTIVE _____

People who use _____ a lot have come up with their
PLURAL NOUN

own way to _____ certain expressions. Since I'm on
VERB

my computer _____ hours a day, I've _____ the most
NUMBER   VERB (PAST TENSE)

_____ ways to use abbreviations. I _____
ADJECTIVE   VERB

using "BBL", which means "Be Back Later." Doesn't it sound

_____? If I'm only going to be away for _____
ADJECTIVE   NUMBER

minutes, I usually tell my friend _____ that I'll "BRB",
CELEBRITY (FEMALE)

which means "Be Right Back." I wouldn't want to keep her

_____. And instead of having to _____
VERB ENDING IN "ING"   VERB

out the entire word "later," you can use the abbreviation "L8R."

_____! My very _____ abbreviation,
EXCLAMATION   ADJECTIVE

however, is "TTFN", which stands for "Ta Ta For Now." Since everyone

on my favorite TV show, *The* _____, says that, I think I
SOMETHING ALIVE

sound as _____ as they do!
ADJECTIVE